THE TOP TEN
EVENTS
THAT CHANGED THE WORLD

Anita Ganeri

PowerKiDS
press.

New York

Published in 2010 by The Rosen Publishing Group, Inc.
29 East 21st Street, New York 10010

Designed and produced by
David West Books

Designer: Gary Jeffrey
Illustrator: David West
Editor: Katharine Pethick
U.S. Editor: Kara Murray

Photographic credits: 7bl, David Friel; 15mt, TMWolf; 11b, 17b, Library of Congress; 20-21 all images courtesy of NASA; 23m, White House Photo Office; 24, Remko van Dokkum; 25mt, U.S. Air Force photo/Capt. Andy Biro; 25m, U.S. Air Force photo/Capt. Patrick Nichols; 25b, Photo by Derek Jensen

Library of Congress Cataloging-in-Publication Data

Ganeri, Anita, 1961–
The top ten events that changed the world / Anita Ganeri. — 1st ed.
p. cm.
Includes index.
ISBN 978-1-4358-9161-6 (library binding) — ISBN 978-1-4358-9162-3 (pbk.) —
ISBN 978-1-4358-9163-0 (6-pack)
1. World history—Juvenile literature. I. Title.
D21.3.G36 2010
909—dc22

2009018052

Printed in China

Contents

Introduction

The following events have been selected as the top ten events from thousands of historical events that have changed our world. It is a very difficult choice to make since there are so many events to pick from. So why have these ten made it into the book and others that seem equally important have not?

✱ First, the event must have affected the entire world, not just a part of it.

✱ Second, it must have had an impact on the world within a reasonably short amount of time. The Ice Age, for example, does not make the top ten because it happened over a longer period of time.

The Ice Age is an example of an important event that affected most of our world. Unfortunately, it also unfolded too slowly to be included in our list.

The San Francisco earthquake and fire of 1906 was a momentous event, but it only directly affected the United States.

The bombing of civilians in Guernica, during the Spanish civil war in 1937, caused outrage but this event has not shaped the modern world.

* Third, it must still affect our lives today in the way it has helped shape the modern world we live in.

You might disagree with the decision to include some of the events that were chosen. In this case, you might like to put together your own list of important events.

The Cretaceous-Tertiary Extinction Event

Around 65 million years ago, dinosaurs roamed the world, the oceans teemed with marine life, and pterosaurs flew through the skies. Then came an event so cataclysmic that 80 percent of all animal species on Earth perished. Many people believe that the cause of this mass extinction was a meteorite, a piece of rock from space that passed through Earth's atmosphere to collide with Earth at very high speed. Such an impact would have sent so much rock and dust into the atmosphere that the whole world would have been plunged into darkness for months.

Proof of the impact is clearly visible in rocks in certain places. This is a layer rich in iridium, a mineral found only in meteorites.

AN EXTINCTION DISASTER

There is much proof to support the idea that the mass extinction was caused by a meteorite strike. A crater more than 112 miles (180 km) in diameter has been discovered in the Yucatán Peninsula, in Mexico. The crater, known as the Chicxulub crater after the present-day town near its center, seems to have been created by an impact 65 million years ago, at the end of the Cretaceous period. The collision of the meteorite also seems to have caused widespread wildfires and tsunamis. All the dinosaurs, except for the archosaurs, disappeared after this time, as did many types of marine life and the pterosaurs, in one of the largest extinctions of all time. The survivors had Earth to themselves.

Pieces from the meteorite may have struck the Moon, causing craters like the Tycho crater, which is clearly visible on the Moon's surface. It is probably the result of an asteroid impact more than 100 million years ago.

Crocodilians, such as this gharial, have evolved from survivors of the mass extinction.

Without competition, early mammals evolved into new animals, such as bats, which filled the empty skies.

Would hominins, which gave rise to humans, have evolved in a dinosaur-dominated world?

Birds are the only living descendants of the dinosaurs.

The Black Death

The early 1300s were hard years for Europe. Food shortages and rising prices resulted in a terrible famine that lasted from 1315 to 1317. Meanwhile a deadly, infectious disease, bubonic plague, was heading toward Europe along the trade routes from the East. In 1347, it reached Crimea, now part of Ukraine, and was then carried further into Europe by traders. The undernourished people of Europe were helpless against it. Victims rarely lived for more than three days after infection. It probably got its name, the Black Death, from the black color of a victim's skin just before death. For three years, it raged in Western Europe, terrorizing towns and wiping out whole communities. The population of Europe was reduced by about one-third and about 25 million people died as a result of the Black Death.

Bubonic plague was a highly infectious disease, caused by a bacterium carried in the blood of fleas that lived on black rats. When the rats died, the fleas bit humans and infected them. Symptoms included fever, vomiting, and swelling.

THE GRIM REAPER

To the survivors of the plague outbreak of 1347 to 1351, the world would never be the same again. Before the Black Death, the feudal system tied peasants to working for a particular landowner. But the high number of plague deaths resulted in a huge labor shortage. Now peasants could choose to work for the highest bidder, bringing the feudal system to an end. The experience of the plague also led to a whole new way of thinking about humanity and its place in the world. People lost faith in the church. They married later, had fewer children, and decided to enjoy life in the moment. In many countries, art reflected people's preoccupation with death and what happened after death.

Plague doctors wore masks and long robes to try to protect themselves from infection.

In 1381, peasants in England rose up in rebellion. They were angry at the king's attempts to take away some of the rights they had gained after the end of the Black Death.

Shown here is a scene from *The Decameron*, completed in 1353, a book of stories inspired by the Black Death.

The Boston Tea Party

On a cold December evening in 1773, a group of around 200 men, some dressed as Indians, headed towards Griffin's Wharf in Boston Harbor. They boarded three tea ships that were anchored there and quickly began to break open the chests of tea that were loaded on the ships. The tea and the chests were dumped over the side into the waters of the harbor. Once the ships were emptied of tea, the men slipped quietly away. This event was called the Boston Tea Party. The actions of the American colonists who dumped the 342 chests of tea were meant to send a clear message to the British government: We will not pay your taxes!

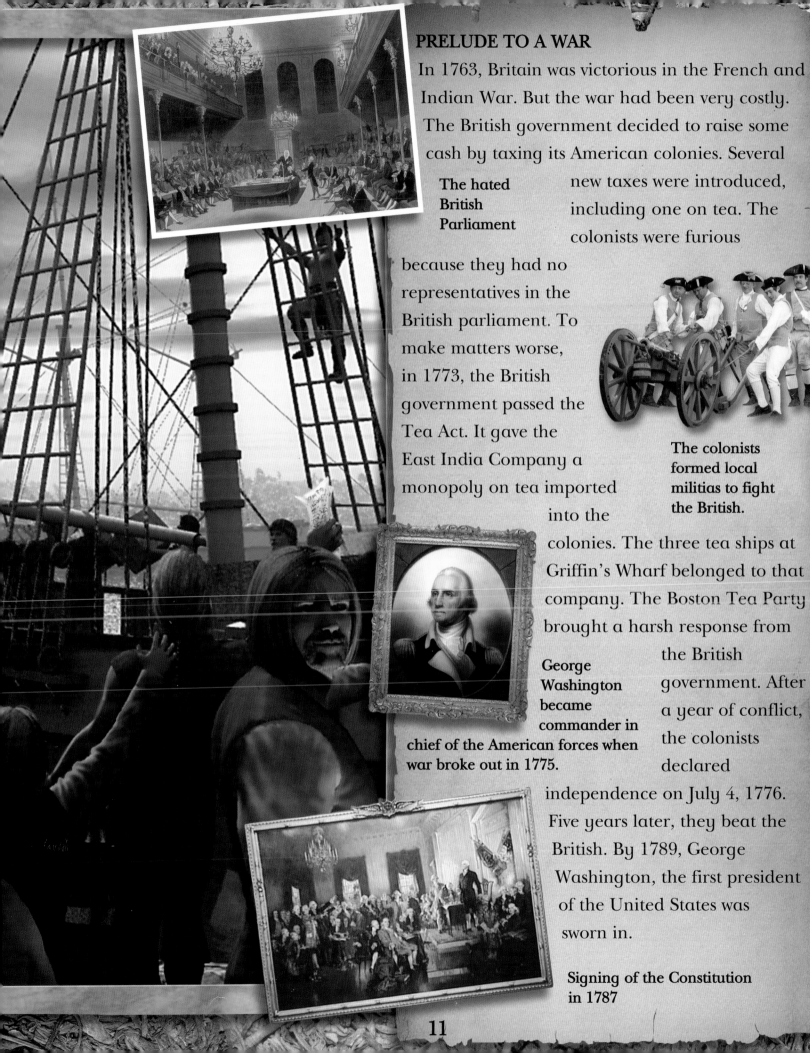

PRELUDE TO A WAR

In 1763, Britain was victorious in the French and Indian War. But the war had been very costly. The British government decided to raise some cash by taxing its American colonies. Several new taxes were introduced, including one on tea. The colonists were furious

The hated British Parliament

because they had no representatives in the British parliament. To make matters worse, in 1773, the British government passed the Tea Act. It gave the East India Company a monopoly on tea imported into the

The colonists formed local militias to fight the British.

colonies. The three tea ships at Griffin's Wharf belonged to that company. The Boston Tea Party brought a harsh response from the British government. After a year of conflict, the colonists declared

George Washington became commander in chief of the American forces when war broke out in 1775.

independence on July 4, 1776. Five years later, they beat the British. By 1789, George Washington, the first president of the United States was sworn in.

Signing of the Constitution in 1787

11

Mount Tambora Eruption

Mount Tambora, on the island of Sumbawa, in Indonesia, was a giant volcano rising 14,108 feet (4,300 m) into the sky. It had been silent for many thousands of years until 1815. On April 5 of that year, people living more than 600 miles (1,000 km) from the volcano reported hearing explosions that sounded like cannon fire. These small eruptions, however, were only warning signs of the cataclysm to come. Six days later, onlookers described seeing "three columns of fire rising to a great height." A huge eruption sent 12 cubic miles (50 cubic km) of magma shooting out of Mount Tambora, plunging Sumbawa and islands hundreds of miles (km) away into darkness. Flows of hot ash and gas streamed down Tambora's slopes at terrifying speeds, burying and burning everything in their path. The ash fell into the sea, setting off tsunamis that engulfed neighboring islands. At least 10,000 people died in the disaster.

The massive eruption took 4,757 feet (1,450 m) off the top of Mount Tambora. The explosion also created a crater 3.7 by 4 miles (6 by 7 km) wide and 1 mile (1 km) deep in the top of the volcano.

Pieces of pumice measuring 8 inches (20 cm) across rained down.

Europe suffered widespread crop failures just as it was recovering from the Napoleonic Wars, fought from 1759 to 1815.

VOLCANIC WINTER

Over 220 million tons (200 million t) of sulphur dioxide gas were launched into Earth's atmosphere as a result of the eruption, reflecting sunlight away from the Earth. Global temperatures fell by as much as 37 °F (3 °C), and 1816 became known as the year without a summer. Snow fell during June and frost was still widespread in July. Many crops failed, causing the worst famine of the 19th century. Hundreds of thousands of people died. People were reduced to eating rats and farmers were murdered by famished mobs as they took their produce to market. The eruption of Mount Tambora was the first modern disaster to affect the entire planet.

In 1991, Mount Pinatubo, in the Philippines, erupted for the first time in 600 years. Around 200,000 people were evacuated before the volcano blew. This eruption did not cause the same destruction as Mount Tambora's did.

The Assassination of Archduke Ferdinand

Two gunshots fired on a June morning in Sarajevo, the capital of Bosnia, helped change the course of history. The shots were fired by 19-year-old Gavrilo Princip, a member of a Serbian revolutionary group, called the Black Hand. He was aiming at Archduke Franz Ferdinand and his wife, Sophie, who were on an official visit to Sarajevo. Having just survived one assassination attempt that day, they were leaving the city when their open-topped car was forced to slow down at a sharp turn. The archduke and his wife were killed almost instantly.

THE GREAT WAR

Archduke Franz Ferdinand was the heir to the throne of Austria-Hungary.

A 1916 German hand grenade

The Black Hand chose him as a target because they were unhappy about Austro-Hungarian influence in the Balkans. However, the assassination gave Austria-Hungary the excuse it wanted to open hostilities against Serbia.

World War I is remembered for its trench warfare in which many thousands of men died.

Austria-Hungary held the Serbian government responsible for the actions of the Black Hand and declared war on Serbia in July 1914. The effects were immediate. Russia was bound by treaty to come to Serbia's aid, and it mobilized its army. Germany declared war on Russia. France and Britain both declared war on Germany. World War I had started, sparked by Princip's fateful shots.

War machines advanced quickly, giving rise to the world's first fighter aircraft and tanks.

THE
TREATY OF PEACE
of the
THE ALLIED AND ASSOCIATED POWERS
AND
GERMANY,

The Protocol annexed thereto, the Agreement respecting the military occupation of the territories of the Rhine,

AND THE
TREATY
BETWEEN
FRANCE AND GREAT BRITAIN
RESPECTING
Assistance to France in the event of unprovoked aggression by Germany.

Signed at Versailles, June 28th, 1919.

(With Maps and Signatures in facsimile)

Adolf Hitler

No other war changed the map of Europe so much. The peace treaty that ended the war also sowed the seeds for World War II.

Pearl Harbor

It was 7:55 a.m. on a peaceful Sunday morning at the U.S. Command Center on Ford Island, in Pearl Harbor, Hawaii. Commander Logan C. Ramsey spotted the approach of a low-flying plane, then he saw "something black fall out of that plane." It was a bomb. Immediately, Ramsey radioed a message to every U.S. ship and base—"Air raid on Pearl Harbor"—but it was already too late. The Japanese attack on the U.S. naval base at Pearl Harbor was a complete surprise and caused utter chaos. In only two hours, two waves of bombing destroyed a large part of the U.S. Pacific Fleet as well as more than 180 aircraft and left around 2,300 people dead.

A GIANT AWAKENS

Trouble between the United States and Japan had increased when Japan became allies with the Axis powers (Germany and Italy) in 1940. The attack on Pearl Harbor was meant to cripple the U.S. Pacific Fleet and to open up the way for Japan's invasion of Southeast Asia. Before Pearl Harbor, the majority of the U.S. population did not want the United States to join the war between the Allies (Britain, France, and the Soviet Union) and the Axis powers. But the attack caused a huge swing in public opinion. The next day, the United States declared war on Japan, prompting Germany to declare war on the United States. The attack on Pearl Harbor brought the United States into World War II.

This wartime propaganda poster urged the American people to remember the Pearl Harbor attacks.

President Franklin D. Roosevelt signed the declaration of war against Japan the day after the Pearl Harbor attacks.

The American air force joined the Allies in the fight against the Axis powers in Europe and elsewhere.

American troops helped liberate Paris, France, from German control in 1945.

Hiroshima

Early on the morning of August 6, 1945, the B-29 bomber *Enola Gay* took off from the island of Tinian, in the West Pacific. The pilot, Colonel Paul Tibbets, set a course for the city of Hiroshima, in Japan. On board his plane, he had the most powerful bomb known to humans, an

The human cost of conquering islands like Iwo Jima showed that the Japanese army would fight to the bitter end, for years if necessary.

atomic bomb with the code name Little Boy. Tibbets took the bomber up to 31,000 feet (9,500 m) above the city before dropping the bomb at 8:15 a.m. The bomb took about 50 seconds to reach its detonation height, roughly 2,000 feet (600 m) above the city. The explosion rocked the *Enola Gay*, which was already several miles (km) away and sent a huge mushroom cloud up into the air. It destroyed 4 square miles (10 sq km) of the city and instantly killed about 66,000 people. Thousands more died later from radiation poisoning.

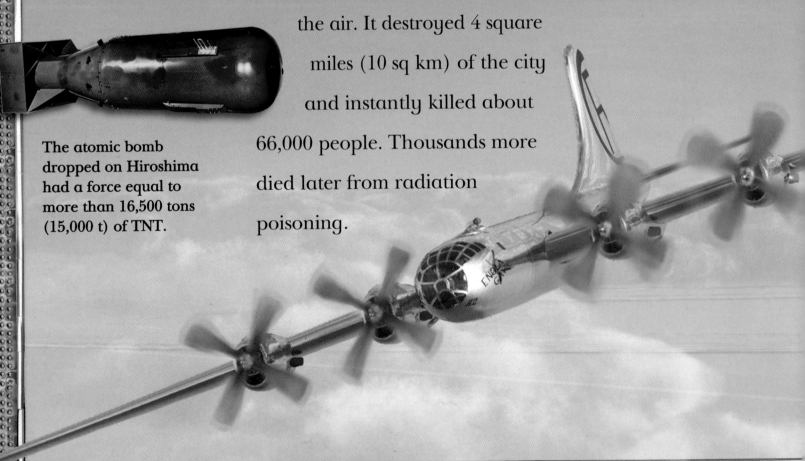

The atomic bomb dropped on Hiroshima had a force equal to more than 16,500 tons (15,000 t) of TNT.

NUCLEAR DAWN

World War II in Europe had finally ended on May 8, 1945. But it was not finished in the Pacific. British and American forces continued to fight the Japanese. The United States, however, had a secret and devastating weapon. The atomic bomb was first tested in July 1945, and the bombing of Hiroshima was the first use of a nuclear weapon. On August 15, Japan finally surrendered, bringing World War II to an end. Hiroshima ushered in the nuclear age, which saw the beginning of the cold war and promised cheap, renewable energy for the future.

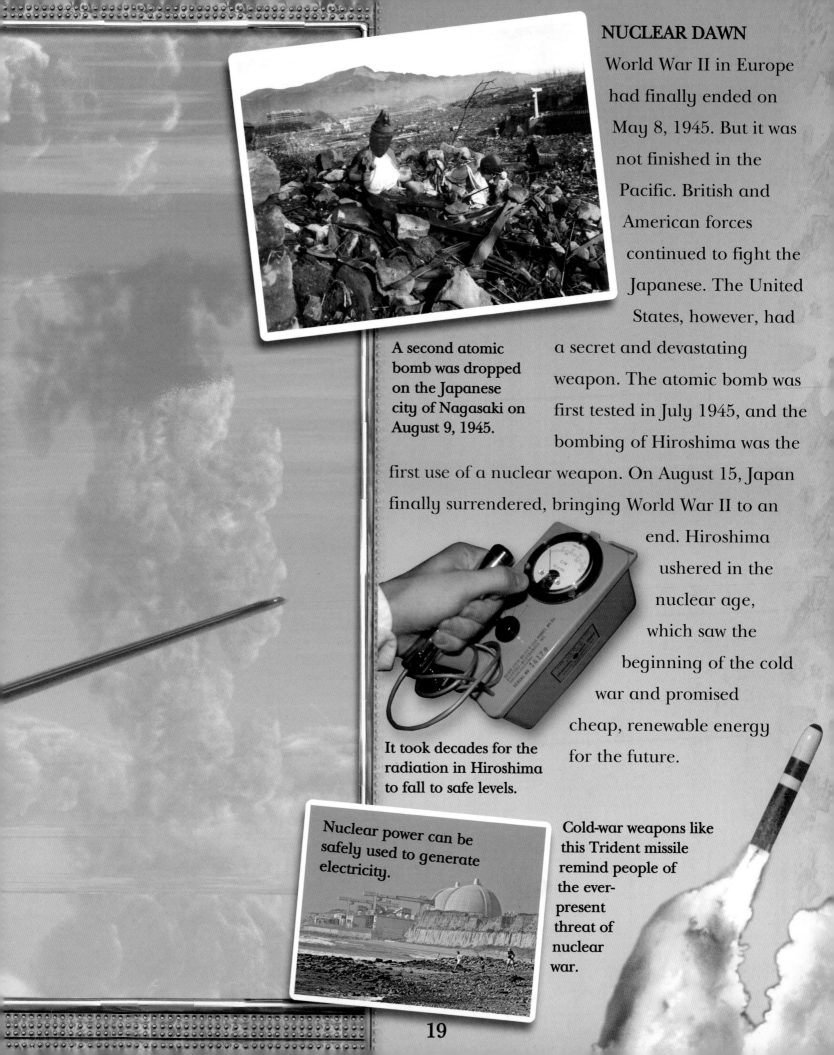

A second atomic bomb was dropped on the Japanese city of Nagasaki on August 9, 1945.

It took decades for the radiation in Hiroshima to fall to safe levels.

Nuclear power can be safely used to generate electricity.

Cold-war weapons like this Trident missile remind people of the ever-present threat of nuclear war.

The Moon Landing

"I believe this nation should commit itself to achieving the goal, before this decade is out, of landing a man on the Moon and returning him safely to the Earth." These words were spoken by President John F. Kennedy in a speech in May 1961. President Kennedy was killed two years later, but his dream was realized in 1969, when the Eagle lunar lander touched down on the surface of the Moon. About 500 million people all over the world watched on their TV screens as astronaut Neil Armstrong took the first step onto the dusty lunar surface, uttering the famous words: "That's one small step for [a] man, one giant leap for mankind."

The last Moon landing, Apollo 17 in 1972, made use of a lunar rover vehicle.

THE SPACE RACE

The Moon landing was a victory for the United States in the space race between the United States and the USSR. The Soviets had successfully launched the first satellite, *Sputnik 1*, into space in 1957 and had put the first man, Yuri Gagarin, into orbit around Earth in 1961. However, after the success of the Apollo 11 mission, international cooperation began to become a feature of space exploration. In 1975, the United States and the USSR launched a joint Apollo-Soyuz mission. Since then, astronauts of many different nationalities have visited the International Space Station. The Moon landing made the dream of space exploration a reality.

The Soviet satellite *Sputnik 1* was launched in 1957.

The U.S. space shuttle made its first mission in 1981. It was the world's first reusable spacecraft.

The explosion of the space shuttle *Challenger* in 1986 affected public feeling about spaceflight.

SpaceShipOne was the first privately funded spacecraft to make a manned spaceflight.

The construction of the International Space Station has been ongoing since 1998.

The Fall of the Berlin Wall

Since 1961, the wall built across the city of Berlin had kept families and friends from each other. Thousands of people had risked their lives crossing the wall from East to West Germany. Many had been captured or killed in the attempt. But in the autumn of 1989, things began to change. On November 9, the East German government lifted the near-total ban on travel to West Germany. Huge crowds of people gathered along the wall, demanding to be allowed through the crossing points. One by one, the gates were opened and crowds of East Germans streamed through. Many people climbed onto the hated wall. Others began to remove chunks from it. The Berlin wall had fallen.

U.S. and Soviet tanks face each other at Checkpoint Charlie, just two months after the construction of the Berlin wall started in 1961.

DIVIDED WE FALL

When World War II ended in 1945, Berlin became a focus for the cold-war conflicts between the Communist Soviet and Western powers. In 1949, Germany was divided into the Communist-controlled German Democratic Republic (East Germany) and the Federal Republic of Germany (West Germany). Over the next few years, thousands of people left East Germany for the West. East Germany gradually closed its borders, until Berlin became the only route to the West. The Berlin wall was built to stop people from leaving. Its destruction came as a result of the political changes of the late 1980s. Soviet leader Mikhail Gorbachev brought in social and economic reforms called perestroika. After 42 years, Germany was reunited.

The cold war, which had brought the world to the edge of destruction, finally ended in 1991.

The Berlin airlift brought supplies to the people of the Western-controlled sectors of Berlin during the Soviet blockade of 1948–9.

Soviet leader Mikhail Gorbachev (right) and U.S. president Ronald Reagan

This Soviet postage stamp promotes the idea of perestroika, which means "restructuring or reform."

Driving humble Trabants, thousands of East Germans crossed into West Germany after the fall of the wall.

9/11

On a cloudless day in New York City, onlookers stood stunned and shocked. At 8:46 a.m. on September 11, 2001, a large plane flew directly into the north tower of the World Trade Center. At first, people were unsure whether they had witnessed an accident. But when a second plane crashed into the south tower only 15 minutes later, it became clear that these were planned attacks. In fact, four planes had been hijacked that morning by 19 attackers, all connected with the fundamentalist Islamic terrorist group al-Qaeda. The third plane hit the headquarters of the U.S. Department of Defense, the Pentagon, at 9:40 a.m. A little later, a fourth plane crashed in a field in Pennsylvania. It seems that its passengers, aware of what was happening, had tried to overpower their attackers.

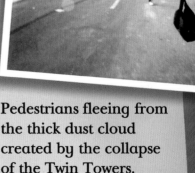

Pedestrians fleeing from the thick dust cloud created by the collapse of the Twin Towers.

THE WAR ON TERROR

Nearly 3,000 people died in the 9/11 attacks. The attacks were condemned by people all around the world, many of whom had watched in disbelief as the horrific events unfolded on their television screens. The attacks soon had far-reaching consequences for countries far from the United States. The fight against terrorism became a top priority for President George Bush, and the search for members of al-Qaeda intensified. The headquarters of al-Qaeda was in Afghanistan. When the Taliban government, which ruled Afghanistan, refused to cooperate with the United States or to hand over the leader of al-Qaeda, Osama bin Laden, U.S. and allied forces launched the invasion of Afghanistan in October 2001. Since 9/11, terrorism has become a grave danger around the world.

President George W. Bush announces the U.S. response to the terrorist attacks.

Fires still raged at Ground Zero, the place where the Twin Towers collapsed, three days after the attack.

The U.S. military began the war in Afghanistan with bombing raids.

Two beams of light showed where the Twin Towers stood in this 2004 memorial.

25

The Best of the Rest

THE FIRST CRUSADE, 1095

An illuminated manuscript shows a scene from the First Crusade.

The Crusades were military campaigns organized by Christian Europe. The Christians wanted to stop the spread of Islam and to recapture the Holy Land, a region that included many places sacred to Christians, from Muslim control. The First Crusade began after Pope Urban II called on Christians to fight a war against the Turks. After three years, the Christians finally succeeded in capturing Jerusalem. The Crusades went on for another 200 years and changed European society forever. They encouraged trade and slowed the advance of Muslim power.

THE FRENCH REVOLUTION, 1789

In 1789, the people of France rose up against their king, Louis XVI. The French peasants were heavily taxed and angry. A disastrous harvest in 1788 had left many hungry. On July 14, a crowd attacked the Bastille prison in Paris, a symbol of the power of the king. In August, the French National Assembly passed the Declaration of the Rights of Man and of the Citizen, which promised the French people that they would now be citizens, not subjects of a monarch. The king was beheaded in 1793. The Revolution led to six years of civil war.

Model of a revolutionary-era guillotine

THE HAITIAN REVOLUTION, 1791

At the time of the French Revolution, Saint-Domingue, an island in the Caribbean, was France's most profitable colony, producing 40 percent of the world's sugar. Its sugar plantations were worked by black slaves from West Africa. In 1791, there was a slave revolt on the island during which a former slave named Toussaint l'Ouverture emerged as a leader. In 1801, Toussaint declared himself governor of the island. But Napoleon Bonaparte sent troops to reclaim the island. In 1804, the French forces were beaten and Saint-Domingue became the independent republic of Haiti.

THE SINKING OF THE *LUSITANIA*, 1915

On May 1, 1915, the British ocean liner *Lusitania* left Pier 54 in New York City, carrying nearly 2,000 passengers heading to Liverpool, England. Many passengers were nervous since Britain was at war with Germany and the Germans had declared the waters around Britain a war zone. On May 7, the *Lusitania* was hit by a torpedo fired by a German U-boat and sank in 20 minutes off the south coast of Ireland. Of the 1,198 lives lost, 128 were U.S. citizens. The sinking of the liner caused outrage in the United States and was one of the reasons for the entry of the United States into World War I in 1917.

The sinking of the *Lusitania* was considered an outrage. The killing of prominent American citizens by the Germans had a powerful effect.

This painting depicts the Haitian revolution. It was the first time slaves had revolted successfully for a lasting freedom.

THE REVOLUTION OF 1917

The Russian Revolution was really two revolutions. The first, in February 1917, overthrew the tsar, and the second, in October, put a Bolshevik, or Communist, in power. In World War I, the Russian army suffered terribly in campaigns against Germany. At home the Russian people were suffering food shortages. A revolt forced Tsar Nicholas II to abdicate, or step down. The provisional government was then overthrown by the Bolshevik Party, led by Vladimir Lenin. The revolution led to civil war and finally to the creation of the Soviet Union.

Vladimir Lenin, leader of the October revolution

THE WALL STREET CRASH, 1929

During the 1920s, the value of stocks and shares in the United States kept rising. Many people used their savings or borrowed money to buy and sell stocks and shares to make a profit. In September 1929, the price of stocks and shares began to go down, and suddenly, people had to sell their investments. October 24, known as Black Thursday, saw the start of a huge rush to sell, which led the market to crash as stocks and shares lost nearly half of their value. This was the start of the Great Depression, during which companies had to close and thousands of people were out of work. It lasted for 10 years and affected countries worldwide.

A victim of the Great Depression

THE CUBAN MISSILE CRISIS, 1962

The missile crisis was a major confrontation between the United States and the USSR. The USSR supported the Communist regime of Fidel Castro in Cuba. In July 1962, the Soviets began to ship ballistic missiles to Cuba, to help defend the island. If fired from Cuba, the missiles could have hit the United States in minutes. President John F. Kennedy set up a blockade to prevent the Soviets from bringing more missiles. Conflict between the two superpowers grew and the world was on the edge of nuclear war until Soviet leader Nikita Khrushchev withdrew the missiles.

The United States shows evidence of Cuban missiles to the United Nations.

MARTIN LUTHER KING JR.'S WASHINGTON SPEECH, 1963

"I have a dream that one day this nation will rise up and live out the true meaning of its creed: 'We hold these truths to be self-evident, that all men are created equal.'" More than 200,000 people heard the civil rights activist Martin Luther King speak these words as part of his most famous speech.

King's speech was a rallying cry for racial equality and justice.

King's "I have a dream" speech took place in Washington D.C., on August 28, 1963. The March on Washington was organized to demand equal justice for citizens of all races. Martin Luther King was killed by an assassin's bullet in 1968.

THE IRANIAN REVOLUTION, 1979

In January 1978, Iran was rocked by protests against its monarch, Shah Mohammad Reza Pahlavi. Many protesters supported the Islamic cleric Ayatollah Khomeini, who had been in exile since 1964.

The effects of the Iranian revolution are still being felt today.

The protests and strikes continued despite government efforts to stop them. In January 1979, the shah was forced to flee the country. Two weeks later, crowds welcomed Ayatollah Khomeini back to Iran. Government troops were overthrown and Khomeini declared Iran to be an Islamic Republic.

THE INDIAN OCEAN EARTHQUAKE, 2004

On December 26, 2004, an underwater earthquake off the coast of Sumatra, in Indonesia, set off an enormous tsunami. Over the next 7 hours, the series of huge waves traveled thousands of miles (km) across the Indian Ocean, devastating coastal areas when they made landfall. This catastrophic tsunami killed at least 225,000 people in Indonesia, Sri Lanka, India, the Maldives, and Thailand.

Sumatra was one of many countries devastated by the 2004 tsunami.

THE WORLD FINANCIAL CRISIS, 2008

The financial crisis began in 2007, when house prices in the United States dropped rapidly. This then affected banks, mortgage lenders, and insurance companies. Many businesses, which could no longer borrow money from their ailing banks, collapsed. The crisis spread around the world. In 2008, stock markets crashed and banks were bailed out by governments. The resulting recession was the worst since the 1930s.

Timeline of Events

		The Event	What Happened
PREHISTORY	65 million years ago	THE CRETACEOUS–TERTIARY EXTINCTION EVENT	It is thought that a meteorite hit Earth, creating a dust cloud that blocked out the Sun.
	2.6 million years ago	THE ICE AGE	Ice sheets and glaciers covered large parts of Earth's surface.
ANCIENT	3000 B.C.	EGYPT IS UNIFIED	Lower and Upper Egypt became a unified state.
	753 B.C.	ROME IS FOUNDED	According to some legends, this is the founding date of the city of Rome.
MEDIEVAL	1347	THE BLACK DEATH	The plague was carried along trade routes from Asia to Europe, reaching Europe in 1347.
	1493	THE DISCOVERY OF THE NEW WORLD BY CHRISTOPHER COLUMBUS	Italian sailor Christopher Columbus sailed west from Spain across the Atlantic Ocean.
MODERN	1773	THE BOSTON TEA PARTY	American colonists dumped cargoes of tea into Boston Harbor in protest over taxes.
	1789	THE FRENCH REVOLUTION	The French people overthrew the royal family.
	1815	MOUNT TAMBORA	The volcano erupted, killing 10,000 people instantly and 82,000 as a result of ashfall.
20TH CENTURY–	1914	THE ASSASSINATION OF ARCHDUKE FERDINAND	Gavrilo Princip assassinated Archduke Franz Ferdinand and his wife, Sophie, in Sarajevo.
	1917	THE RUSSIAN REVOLUTION	The tsar was overthrown by Bolshevik power.
	1929	THE WALL STREET CRASH	The value of stocks dropped suddenly.
	1941	PEARL HARBOR	The Japanese attacked the U.S. Pacific Fleet in Pearl Harbor, Hawaii.
	1945	HIROSHIMA	A U.S. B-29 bomber dropped the first atomic bomb on the Japanese city of Hiroshima.
	1963	THE CUBAN MISSILE CRISIS	Soviet plans for missiles in Cuba caused conflict between the United States and the USSR.
	1969	THE APOLLO 11 MOON LANDING	Neil Armstrong was the first man on the Moon.
	1989	THE FALL OF THE BERLIN WALL	Crossing points in the Berlin wall were opened.
	2001	THE 9/11 TERROR ATTACKS	Al-Qaeda terrorists hijacked planes and flew two into New York's Twin Towers.
	2004	INDIAN OCEAN EARTHQUAKE	A powerful earthquake set off a huge tsunami.

What Changed

The event killed off the dinosaurs.
The world's climate was cooler and drier than the climate today.
The dynastic period in Egyptian history began.
The ancient Romans built a powerful empire.
The plague killed one-third of Europe's population.
The "discovery" of the New World opened up the Americas to European exploration.
The British government's response helped set the British and colonists on the path to war.
The Revolution resulted in civil war, which ended when Napoleon Bonaparte seized power.
The eruption affected the world climate, causing the "year without a summer" (1816).
The assassination set in motion a series of events that led to the start of World War I.
The revolution led to the formation of the USSR.
The crash resulted in the Great Depression.
The attack brought the United States into World War II.
After a second bomb was dropped on Nagasaki, the Japanese surrendered, ending World War II.
The world was on the edge of nuclear war until the USSR backed down.
This encouraged investment in space science.
East and West Germany were united again.
President Bush launched the war on terror against al-Qaeda in Afghanistan.
225,000 died and coastal areas were devastated.

Glossary

atomic bomb (uh-TAH-mik BOM) A weapon that explodes as a result of nuclear fission.

Balkans (BAWL-kunz) The countries that lie in the Balkan peninsula in southeast Europe.

cold war (KOLD WOR) The state of conflict that existed between the United States and the USSR from the mid-1940s until the early 1990s.

extinction (ek-STINK-shun) The state of no longer existing.

feudal system (FYOO-dul SIS-tem) The medieval system that tied peasants to work for a particular manor and lord.

militias (muh-LIH-shuz) Military forces made up of citizens.

monopoly (muh-NO-puh-lee) A situation in which a person or a business has sole control over a particular service or product.

outrage (OWT-rayj) Very angry feelings.

propaganda (pro-puh-GAN-duh) Information aimed at affecting the way people think and behave.

space race (SPAYS RAYS) The race between the United States and the USSR to be the first in space.

torpedo (tor-PEE-doh) A self-propelled weapon that can be fired through the air or under water and is made to explode on impact.

tsunamis (soo-NAH-meez) Giant waves caused by the movement of undersea earthquakes.

Index

Web Sites

Due to the changing nature of Internet links, PowerKids Press has developed an online list of Web sites related to the subject of this book. This site is updated regularly. Please use this link to access the list:
www.powerkidslinks.com/topt/events/